LEAVING
EARTH

LEAVING EARTH

poems

DJ Hills

Split Rock Press
Washburn, Wisconsin
2022

ISBN 978-1-7354839-4-8

Cover art: DJ Hills and Crystal S. Gibbins
Layout design: Crystal S. Gibbins

Split Rock Press Chapbook Series readers: Amy Clark, Violeta Garcia-Mendoza, Crystal S. Gibbins, Whitney (Walters) Jacobson, Andrew Jones

Split Rock Press is dedicated to publishing eco-friendly books that explore place, environment, and the relationship between humans and the natural world. Visit us online at www.splitrockreview.org/press.

Environmental consciousness is important to us. This book is printed with chlorine-free ink and acid-free paper stock supplied by a Forest Stewardship Council certified provider. The paper stock is made from 30% post-consumer waste recycled material.

For my family – given and found

TABLE OF CONTENTS

NOSTALGIA

The sun feels smaller now.
Wind whistles through the cracks
in the window and curls up beside me in bed.
I dream of the days I got drunk
at your aunt's Fourth of July picnic

and cried on the drive home
because you wouldn't hold my hand;
when the afternoons were long and unbearable
and didn't trip over one another in haste;

when the distance between us could be measured
by a string and two tin cans. The world was no bigger
than the gaps between our fingers

and even the traffic outside my window
rushed past with a homesick familiarity.

LEAVING HAGERSTOWN

When you reach the city a car alarm
will sound like a memory you had
once but are already forgetting:
a few bodies you knew, a joint passed
between familiar hands, laughter,
a screeching, singing car. Whose?

Only after trading these mortal coils
will you see how beautiful they are:
the rivers and the creek beds bursting with life;
the streets you memorized without trying;
the mountains gathering their towns like a mother
gathers her children in from playing;

and the cars, of course; the cars and the bodies
who filled them; the cars and the car alarms;
hands outstretched in tag; the gentlest touch
that sets cars blazing.

HOME TOUR

I am a restless tour guide, overeager
to share every mundane fact of my life.
As though you have never seen a swing set,
a river, the spectacular mediocrity
of youth. You take the stories in stride;
nodding as I peel back each layer,
unearthing more story, a compounding saga.
Every tree here has its memories; every stone
a bit of my blood. I am clumsy and desperate for you
to fall in love with even the hazy blue of the mountains.

PUBERTY POEM

I'd forgotten all of it until now:
his dark hair, my dark hair,
the hair on my legs sprouting like moss
on the trees; our skin wet with sweat
from running through the trees; the slant
of the sun as it fell between the trees;
the anxious way we dressed behind different trees;
the later way we searched for conversation
under the needled floor; the gash on his foot
pumping blood onto the kitchen floor; his mom:
What did you need to take your shoes off for?

WAYNESBORO, PA

It is dark in Pennsylvania. In Pennsylvania there are stars.

On the road home a barn still boasts

a Trump 2020 sign.

People find God in Pennsylvania.

I look along the riverbank

but find only crawfish. I am young

in Pennsylvania. In Pennsylvania I do not drink.

I kissed a boy in Pennsylvania.

We had sex along a riverbank

near an old barn. We drank

from each other, our names screamed like boasts.

God gave us privacy but the stars

watched, every wink a sign

of something more. When I was young

there was nothing more. All roads led to Pennsylvania.

CUCUMBER FALLS

—for my parents

This place unearths a memory I have that isn't mine.
Here the trees grow close, the forest dark as any mine,

the air botanical with the perfume of rattlesnakes.
Years ago, you sunned yourselves like snakes,

on the same cropping of rocks. Momma would have stayed forever
but you had a schedule and the sun doesn't shine forever.

Today, there is no schedule. You tell us a story I thought I knew:
about visiting Wright's *Fallingwater.* Back then, it still felt new:

uncovering pockets of earth in the cool of October; falling
in love all over again; and around you all the water, falling.

LEAVING LOUISIANA

& when it is all said & done:

when the last strains of bayou sound have faded
to rumble strips when the mountains have risen around you

(& you will forget last names
& you will forget the way home from the grocery store)

you may search for some meaning in the dirt you brought back
you may hum along to accents that you cannot claim

you may ask the rain for help
the sun for warmth   the winter to bring you back

(& you will forget last names
& you will forget the way home from the bar)

& what will you have to say for this?:

the sky looks better fried white with humidity
no one asks about you anymore

that is *are you doing all right?*
or *is there anything you need?*

(& you will forget last names
& you will forget the way home after dark)

& when it is all said & done what will you have to say for this?:

that you loved them   that you loved them
relentlessly   that they loved you restlessly

(& you will forget last names
& you will forget the way home from the mailbox)

& when is it done? & what will you say?

& all is this & this:
roads that will never be paved

blue street signs
skin & beer

& the sound of voices you cannot claim

THE GNO BRIDGE

We pull into the overlook, eyes peeled
for trouble, and Sawyer keeps the van
running in case we have to *get out fast.*

The Westbank faces us, more or less
dark; the bridge the brightest thing
around except, maybe, the headlights

casting our shadows into the river
like drowning victims. Greasy foam
builds up around anything solid in the water:

boats or sticks or memories.
Sawyer points across the river.
We used to fish there.

Back when this was all woods.
It was a different city then.
Not better, not necessarily.

The air is heavy with the hot, wet breath
of summer. Sawyer has an eye on some folks
on the swing down the Riverwalk *just in case.*

I guess the good thing about being a tourist
is that you can see the city
for everything it could be:

A city without memory.
In that version everyone is smiling
and no one is holding a gun.

In that version every dad on the Westbank
is alive and well. There are trees
in that city and hours to spend fishing.

FUNERAL POEM

Here it is:
    the gun and the needle
        and the needle and the needle.

I can show you
    The smoking gun. I can
        show you the noose and the body swinging.

Whisper overdose
    like an elegy
        and see that it makes no difference.

This hunger for death.
    This row of graves with a shared last name.
        Grief is no warning. Only an invitation.

A license to carry.
    A knot-tying course.
        A needle, a gun, a body to break.

ODE FOR THE LAFAYETTE CEMETERY TOUR GUIDES

Brown skin, polo shirt, and always ready
     with a fact on your lips like a shush
but more polite. *Take a picture, take note*: & etc.
Did you ever consider a career at the bar or McDonald's?
Maybe death pays better: *Another body to gawk at.*
Can't slow down—lots to see.
       Where is home?—like it matters.
As a child did you read guidebooks,
practice walking backwards in the mirror? *Mind your step.*
Mind the dead.—not that they care.
(Right?) *Here we are—all aboard—*
& etc. *Lestat's tomb. We'll rest*
here a while. Check your phone: a text
from a boyfriend you'd like to bury.
Have you fucked on a grave before?
Shall we continue? I'm afraid there's more.
People won't stop dying. But of course
it's all business, no bones about it.
Tourists will believe anything
if they pay you well enough.
       How do you leave them? At the gate
with history they can pocket like postcards.
It is not even noon and no one is listening.
But you have a job to do—tasked with keeping the dead
alive another day longer. Does it follow you,
afterward? Does your boyfriend accuse you
of bringing work home? When he's finished
do you still hear their names?: Theodora,
John, Florence—Trace the dates along
his ribcage: '88, '64, '43. When he asks
do you lie?—*Yes* or *I love you.*

BLUE HERON

A wild gesture of limbs points you out
nearly invisible against the cloudless horizon:

blue as summer, feathers soft and stark
as peat moss. Startled into flight

by the intrusion of orange plastic inner tubes or
the splash of Straw-Ber-Rita cans slipping from drunk grips.

Take me with you! someone calls, as if you would;
as if we have anything to offer in return.

CANTICLE FOR UNIVERSITY PARKS, OXFORD

When the sun finally breaks and the air is soft and muggy enough to swim in
and the sidewalks are cracking from foot traffic and the brutalism of Wolfson
is weighing on the soul you will find us between willows older than God,
along the forearm of the River Cherwell, treading on clean stones
(because nothing here stays dry long enough to dirty), talking about Sylvia Plath
and home and how lonely the buildings look today and wondering
if they ever take a break from their grandeur to just sit and listen.
        Today he is wearing short sleeves for the first time in ages
and I am learning to hate sweaters for the way they have hidden his skin.
        Already he is stealing this place from me. I know it
by the way I am afraid to uncover some rotting leaf for fear of finding him there.
        He is the snipped tail on the dog we love and the ripples from a punt pole;
he is the thrill of the jackhammer two blocks down; the bicycle bell and the loose pram
        wheel; the daisy field and the cricket pitch and the bench where he pauses
to tie his shoe. He is telling me about Sylvia Plath, how he lost her last month
        on a Ryanair plane to Greece. (How he manages to lose everything he loves
right in the middle.) Our path ends at the corner of Parks Road and Norham Gardens
        where every double-decker in Oxford is waiting for us. It is June,
and the last day we will see each other, and the whole city feels like it is coming alive.

21

LEAVING BALTIMORE

When I leave, all that's left to take with me is a desk chair
I didn't buy, a calligraphy pen that never worked,
a pair of briefs red and ripe as a summer tomato.

I only miss places when I look at the receipts I saved by accident,
caught between the pages of books I orphan, unfinished, on the stoop.
Unimart, you knew me best. My late night fantasies. My secret shames.

The floors are dirty, the doorknob is sticky. I leave all of this behind.
Rooms are smallest when they're emptied—we have this in common.
I worry about who will mow the grass when I'm gone. As it were,

cities don't need anyone the way we need them.
I want to call my mechanics and tell them I loved them.
I want to hold hands with the cashier at Eddie's,

who tucked the eggs where they'd be safest from my clumsiness.
I want to remember Greenmount's sidewalks as cracked
as the day they found me, like geriatric bones, the neighborhood

ungentrified. I want to leave behind
a sunny day and discover it still smiling,
when I pass through on my way to somewhere else.

IT'S MONDAY AND I DON'T HAVE HIV

Everything today is beautiful: even the needle in my arm
I can't bear to look at, filling vial after vial until I'm light
enough to float free and careless; the sky this morning exactly
the color of a good morning and every dog pissing on monuments
in gleeful, golden showers; the wild, scorched grass left unchecked
all summer, spreading its roots insatiably beneath the sidewalk;
the very fact that we are here—wasting the better half of an hour
on the stoop outside your apartment, debating the pros and cons
of horror movies—or not debating—agreeing—that we're both
too scared of possession to appreciate the subtle layers of feminist
theory or Jamie Lee Curtis; and meanwhile the blood in our veins
is the descendant of the blood that has always been there,
the exponentially great-grandchild of it, content with its short life,
never even mourning the loss from the needle, or the time I split
my knee open skating, back when I was afraid of kissing
but wanted to be kissed more than anything.

EVERYWHERE IN BALTIMORE LITANIES OF RAVENS

pockmark the sky; and meanwhile I'm afraid
the only pictures I have of you are losing their color
like beach houses with their identical façades—your smile
wasting away in whatever light is left at the end of the season,
until I will be forced to remember you stone-faced and sad—
in another bedroom, in another corner of this Hitchcockian city. And reall·
I wouldn't mind the birds so much if they didn't remind me of you:
their fine feathers and preening; their un-musical voice; the paling
they form along rooftops, reducing me to a passing curiosity, or more likel·
not caring about me at all; marking their days by the sun,
and the sturdy comfort of branches, which might have been
my hands if I could ever learn to stand so still.

LOOKING

I. Host

I'll remind you that my body is not my own
      Every space I've built was foraged
to fill a lack I cannot name
      In January I climbed out of my skin
to see what was left behind
      A few pinecones thorny with promise
carpeted the ground beneath
      my folded flesh and he gathered the remains
in his arms spinning some wild story
      about the girl who housed them and the gaps between her ribs
that he clung to just to tether me to something
      as I travelled the distance between his pelvis and the sky

II. Travel

I'll remind you that my body is not my own
      Nightly I haunt ratlike
across the city and row home after row home beckons me
      inside I undress from my morals
become *boy* or *bastard*
      Who's your daddy?
        Who's your daddy?
In fairness I've never known Suturing a body together
      is scavenging for truth in a grab bin at Savers
Who's my daddy?
      Any answer I could give is a lie
The loneliest part of the city is where the skyline breaks
      from the sky

IF WE MUST DIE LET IT COME AFTER A LONG EVENING OF LAUGHTER

—after Hanif Abdurraqib

The last night I drove him home, I took a wrong turn,

crisscrossing Baltimore, wondering if he noticed
how many times we'd passed the arboretum.

His eyes were as bright as ever, and his chin
was peppered with the wiry excuse of a beard.

I wanted to tell him—*You got older.*
I hope we both get so, so old.

That evening, he kept starting stories
he couldn't finish and I found myself repeating

It's all right
although he didn't ask.

It isn't enough to wish for him
a story with a happier ending.

As quickly as I found him, he was gone,

tearing on about needing a house and a dog
and a husband to come home to,

frantic as the night I held him down with my palm
over his racing heart, trying to make him understand

he was having a panic attack—not dying—

Although what truth was there between us,
as he leaned back into the car, grinning

and swearing he loved me *more
than anyone*. Swearing that I was his best friend.

He made it easy to smile back,
to tell him whatever he wanted,

and then leave him, beaming after me in the dark.

LEAVING EARTH

1

2

3

4

5

6   7

8

---

[1] Our bones are made of exploded stars.
[2] We are only the shrapnel of brighter things; our names
[3] nothing but a way to mark where we've been.
[4] I go in search of the nameless so that I may be unnamed, too.
[5] I cannot kill a cat to ease its suffering but in childhood I held a corn husk in my small, cruel fist and whipped our family pet until it howled.
[6] (Even in space I am not weightless.
[7] I have brought with me all the colors of fall.)
[8] Impossible to trust any permanent thing keeps the ocean from spilling into the sky.

LOST

Unable to find one's way.
Synonyms: adrift,
like at sea. Like see
how far I've come,
the miles I've swam,
the bridges I've burned.

Denoting something
that has been taken away
or cannot be recovered:
Paper in flames, my voice
in a windstorm,
my aunt's first-born son.

Or a verb: to lose;
as in, I am losing my grip,
as in, I am trying to hold
on but it is all slipping
through the cracks.

Or past: that is,
we had it once
but we lost it.
That is, I've given up
hoping it will ever
come back.

.

THE WASHINGTON POST WONDERS ABOUT LIFE ON VENUS

Last week I could not see the sun
        through the haze of another coast's wildfires.
It feels like I am always calling friends

to see if they have died.
        X Æ A-Xii has gone
to prepare a place for us

and I will take my place
        among the dodos and the dinosaurs.
There is never enough space on the ship.

A fossil is a fossil
        and a bubble of gas
is a prayer.

No one I've asked seems to know
        how many rain cycles it would take
to replace all the water in the sea.

WHILE PARIS BURNS

miles away from any of this
you rest / in tangles of tube and cannula / *it will all be over soon*
a mantra spoken like a promise and not a prayer / recovery is
a word for mouths that do not smolder / buildings without
histories / bodies without histories / let memory be a
monument / doctors feed us weeks intravenously / babel was
razed and now / we speak of ruin in tongues / we do not
understand / we ask for more but / there is only so much /
days crumble like spires / in flames

SMALL COMFORT

—for Dee

Try to remember the vastness of it all: the moon,
for starters; rolls, warm and yeasty, rising in the oven;
the sky under your feet as you rose, high—higher!
—on the swing; the ocean, of course, and the mouths
of everything swimming in it. Tomorrow will come;
for now—catch the germ a child sneezed on the rail
of the afternoon bus (let it fester a cold in you—
let that be all that festers); or a ball—one of the ones
made with rubber and thread—thread the pattern
memory makes through all of this—trace it along
the streams of telephone wires connecting you
to some distant ocean. To be an ocean again—
children understand this better. But you'll be okay—
although some days a little sick (remember
the cold?) and sick—some days—of all of it:
numbers and names and neighborhoods you've lost
but are having trouble forgetting. It will matter less
one day; the vastness contained in the palm of your hand:
a seashell; a child's belief—Listen: today, it's the ocean,
tomorrow, your blood, your beating heart.

UPON LEAVING YOU FOR THE LAST TIME

—after Jonathan Musgrove

This is it, I say, like I've said before,
and I mean it. Like every other time before.

You become sweat stains on a pillow, the smell
of Jim Beam. Every text message and letter

your same incantation: *You're going to miss me.*
You are probably right—you always are.

The leaves keep turning. The river rises.
Spring comes back to Maryland.

This poem is for you. It is the love poem
you begged me to write but I never could.

AFTER A LONG VACATION

—a tanka for Ki

I return sunburnt
salt watered summer tempered
by cheap mojitos

I find you in the kitchen
unchanged I love you for it

ACKNOWLEDGMENTS

Many thanks to the editors who championed these poems, which have previously appeared online or in print, some in slightly altered forms.

"Nostalgia" and "Blue Heron" in *Appalachian Review*

"Leaving Hagerstown," "Puberty Poem," and "Canticle for University Parks, Oxford" in *Apeiron Review*

"The GNO Bridge" in *Arkansas Review*

"If We Must Die Let It Come After a Long Evening of Laughter" in *Free State Review* (Online)

"While Paris Burns" in *Lunch*

"Everywhere in Baltimore Litanies of Ravens" and "Leaving Earth" in *Split Rock Review*

Thank you to the Kratz Center for Creative Writing at Goucher College whose Summer Writing Fellowship supported the writing of some of these poems.

ABOUT THE AUTHOR

DJ Hills is a writer and theatre artist. Connect with them online at www.dj-hills.com.

Made in the USA
Middletown, DE
26 October 2022

13584013R00024